FIT FOR THE GAME
TENNIS

David Lloyd

WARD LOCK

D1295524

Writer: Bob Hammond
Editor: Heather Thomas
Art Director: Al Rockall

Text set in Univers Medium by Halcyon Type & Design Ltd, Ipswich
Printed and bound in Great Britain by Richard Clay Ltd

**British Library Cataloguing in Publication
Data**

Lloyd, David 1948-
  Tennis.
  1. Sports. Physical fitness
  I. Title II. Series
  613.711

  ISBN 0-7063-6937-8

David Lloyd

David Lloyd needs no introduction in the context of International Tennis. He spent 17 years as one of Britain's foremost professionals on the International circuit. He has played many times at Wimbledon and was Doubles specialist in the British Davis Cup team, being ranked in the top 30 in the world.

Highlights of David's playing career include his wins over Nastase, Connors, Kodes and Gottfried, and in the doubles semi-final at Wimbledon.

In latter years as a player, David has worked as a coach and trainer in Canada and in the Netherlands. He was Coach to the British Wightman Cup Team for several years and also Coach to the Israeli National Team.

Upon his retirement from the circuit in 1981, he formed a company which built and ran the first commercially successful indoor tennis club in Britain. Since then he has built two more large indoor clubs, with the construction of three more centres now well under way.

David Lloyd commentates on BBC radio, and also for the ITV and Channel 4 television channels.

Acknowledgements

The author would like to thank the following people for their help in creating this book:

Bob Hammond for assisting with the writing of the book.

Mark Shearman for taking the photographs of all the exercises and drills.

Allsport for providing photographs of tennis stars throughout.

Matt Lawrence, health and fitness instructor, for helping direct the photographs and exercises at the David Lloyd Raynes Park Club.

Scott Lloyd, Jane Williams and Michael Thorn for appearing in the exercise photographs with David Lloyd.

CONTENTS

INTRODUCTION

The art of being a good sportsman – or sportswoman – is to know your capabilities; and then to try to extend them and push yourself even further. However, there is always something left. The champion will always produce an extra effort just when he appears 'spent'. That is what makes the difference between the top player and the also-ran.

That ability to drag up hidden reserves of strength and energy is a combination of mind and body. Physical fitness and mental fitness go hand-in-hand. In sport they are inseparable. The player who has done a lot of training, who has pushed himself to the limit, will have the mental strength needed in a crisis. He knows that he can still be running hard at the end of the final set, so he can concentrate fully on his game.

The player who has not trained hard, who is not fully fit, will always have that knowledge at the back of his mind. He will be worrying about whether he can last the pace. He may be looking for ways to win

FIT FOR THE GAME: TENNIS

the match quickly, which could produce errors.

It is clear that the dedication to push yourself in training, day after day, itself requires mental toughness. To go out for a five-mile run every day in cold, wet weather, demands mental discipline. The champion can do it, and enjoys doing it. He knows that it is an essential part of getting to the top – and staying there. The player who finds an excuse to duck training for any reason is the player who will struggle to last the pace, physically and mentally, in a tight match. The discipline required to train hard is the same as that needed in matchplay, to stay focused on the game plan, and to hit the right shots every time under pressure.

Every professional player these days devotes time to fitness training. It is simply impossible to survive without it at the top level. Talent alone is not enough. Perhaps thirty years ago it was possible to be a top player without being an athlete, but not any more. Modern equipment enables the ball to be hit harder than ever. Therefore players have to be faster and stronger to be able to chase the balls down. This principle applies at every level of the game.

That is what makes tennis such a wonderful sport. Success requires a combination of many factors: talent, technique, stamina, speed, strength, flexibility and agility, to name the obvious ones. The best players need all those assets plus guts, determination and intelligence.

Boris Becker, Ivan Lendl, Stefan Edberg and Steffi Graf, for instance, have all those qualities to some degree. Edberg is a wonderful athlete – quick, agile, supple and strong, with good racket skills and technique. Graf is similar. Becker is less of an athlete, but compensates for this with raw

Stefan Edberg (opposite) and Ivan Lendl (above) are both extremely fit, but whereas Lendl has to work hard to stay fit, Edberg is fast, powerful and very mobile on court – a natural athlete, in fact.

power and great determination. Ivan Lendl is not a natural athlete but has worked unbelievably hard on his fitness, and his technique, to make up for it.

But don't get the idea that it's only the professional player who will benefit from a greater level of fitness. I can guarantee that the average club player can improve his or

7

her game dramatically by spending some time on fitness training.

A daily routine of press-ups and sit-ups to strengthen stomach and arm muscles, would do wonders for the club player's serve. A daily run would make all the difference in a long match, both to stamina and confidence.

Increased fitness means a slowing down of the heart-beat under exercise. A slower heart-beat means greater control of strokes, and greater clarity of thought under pressure. Slack muscles tighten up under stress, restricting movement.

The former Australian Davis Cup captain, and coach, Harry Hopman, was probably the man who began the fitness drive in tennis. He really put his players through the mill. I remember the former Wimbledon Champion, Lew Hoad, telling me that after a day's training with Hopman, most players were too tired to even lift an arm to comb their hair. Hoad, Ken Rosewall, Frank Sedgman and company ruled the tennis world for years in the 1950s until everyone else began to work just as hard off court.

Now every top player has a fitness programme, and indeed many have their own personal trainers in attendance on the circuit. The club player doesn't need that. An hour or so, three or four days a week, would bring huge benefits. Even a few minutes a day would make a difference.

I hope that the following chapters will provide some ideas and encouragement

Above: Boris Becker is tremendously powerful with a mighty serve. His great athletic ability has helped him to become one of the best players ever.

for tennis players of any level, no matter how much, or how little, time they want to devote to fitness training.

For seventeen years I trained nearly every single day. I loved it, and I still benefit from the basic strength and stamina that fitness work established for me. I hope that everyone reading this book will gain as much. I know that every minute spent on physical training will help your game on court.

Opposite: Steffi Graf is another natural athlete to whom fitness comes easily. Unlike many women players, she has strength, on-court speed and agility in addition to good technique and skill.

CHAPTER ONE

WARMING UP

Walk into the locker room at Wimbledon, or any top tournament, and the scene will be the same: players stretched out on the floor, or on the massage table; or standing with one foot raised on to the table. Warming up is the name of the game. Players are spending more time than ever before on loosening and stretching muscles before going out on court. It has become almost a religion.

It is important for sportsmen to have 'long' muscles. That means a lot of stretching, particularly of the hamstrings. But every muscle group should be properly warmed up before any serious exercise, whether it is a match or a training session. The importance of warming up cannot be over-emphasised.

Cold or 'short' muscles are prone to injury when put under stress. Muscle strains and pulls can be minimized by thorough warm-up routines – and by warming down after the session. For tennis players, ten to fifteen minutes warming up before attempting to hit a ball is a protection against chronic shoulder trouble. Trying to hit serves or overheads before loosening up the shoulder muscles is an invitation to long-term muscle or tendon injury.

A good way to start warming up is to gently jog for a few minutes around the tennis court. Stay loose and relaxed. Don't be tempted into a race if you are working out with a partner. Five or six circuits of a single court should get the blood circulating around the whole body. After three or four laps of normal jogging, put in some sideways steps, alternating between

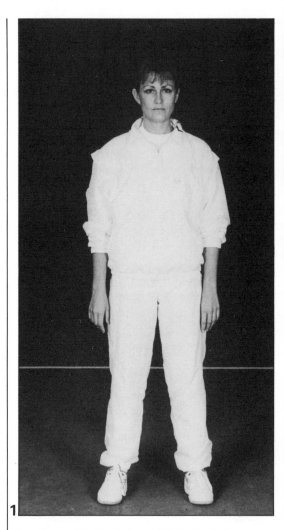

1

leading with the left and right foot, to warm up the different muscles on the inside and outside of the thighs.

Skipping is also a good warm-up exercise, because again most of the muscle groups are brought into action. You can

continued on page 12

The windmill

This is excellent for stretching and loosening the shoulders.

1 Stand upright, hands by the sides.

2 Swing one arm forwards, up and right round in a circle. Try to brush the ear as the arm comes over. Do 5 repetitions.

3 Repeat with the other arm. Round off the exercise by another set of repetitions with both arms together.

gradually increase the time you skip and the pace as you get fitter.

Having got the circulation going, move on to a series of loosening and stretching exercises to cover the most important muscles you will use when playing the game.

Tricep stretch

1 Begin in the upright position, and raise right arm with elbow pointing outwards. Place the fingertips at the base of the head.
2 Slowly cross the hands and push back against the right elbow. Try to get the fingers to crawl down the back as far as possible. Hold the position for 8-10 seconds. This is also good for loosening the shoulders and stretching the tricep muscles on the back of the upper arms.

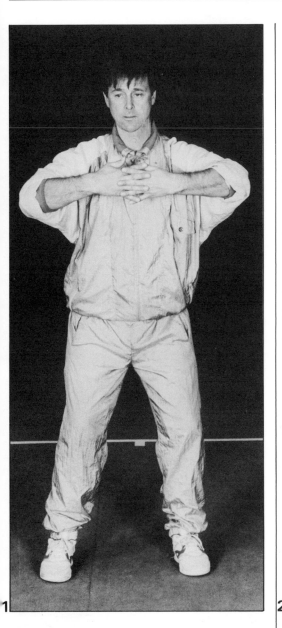

Trunk turns

1 Stand with feet apart, and knees slightly bent. Raise the arms out in front at shoulder height, and turn the head and upper body to one side as far as possible.

2 Hold the position for a few seconds, and then swing slowly right round to the other side, keeping the legs and hips still. Repeat 5 times. This exercise lubricates the spine and torso.

13

Side bends

1 Stand upright, with knees slightly bent, hands by the sides. Raise one arm and extend it upwards above your head.

2 Slowly ease the other hand down the side of the leg, without leaning forwards. Push down as far as possible without straining, supporting your body weight on the thigh, and hold the position for a few seconds. Straighten up, and repeat with the other side. Do 2 repetitions each side. This is helpful in stretching the oblique muscles and sides of the chest.

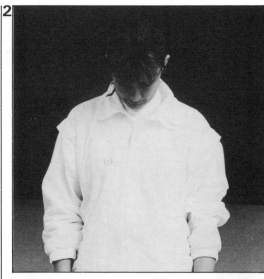

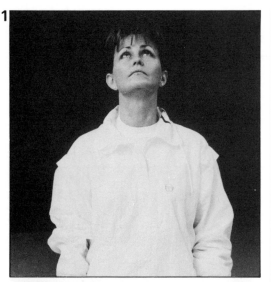

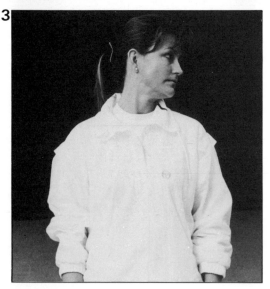

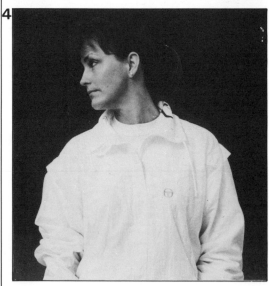

Neck stretches

1 Stand up straight, with the head back, looking up at the sky.

2 Then bring the head slowly forwards and down, until the chin is resting lightly on the chest.

3 Turn the head slowly to one side, and hold for a few seconds.

4 Roll the head back around to the other side, keeping the chin down, and hold again in the extreme position. Repeat 5 times. This exercise is good for keeping the neck loose.

Touching the toes

1 Stand up straight with feet together. Now cross the ankles placing the right foot the other side of the left.

2 Bend from the hips, keeping the legs straight, and ease down with the hands to touch the toes. Hold for 8-10 seconds. Reverse the feet, and repeat on the other side. This exercise will stretch both the lower spine and back muscles and the hamstrings.

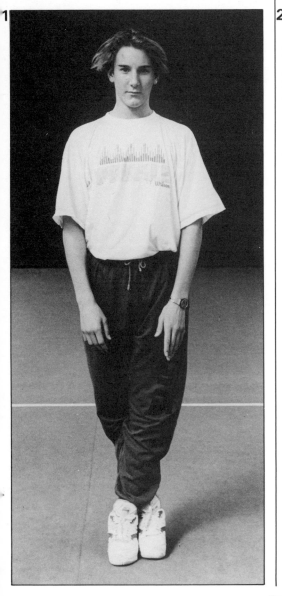

1

Upper back stretch

1 Stand upright, feet shoulder-width apart, and knees slightly bent. Raise your arms to shoulder height, with fingers interlocked, palms facing inwards. Do not lock out your elbows.

2 Pull the arms forward, as if to separate the shoulder blades. Avoid leaning forwards. Hold for 10 seconds. This exercise stretches the trapezius and rhomboid muscles in the upper back region.

Quads stretch

1 Stand upright with feet shoulder-width apart.

2 Raise your right knee, and grasp the right ankle with the right hand.

3 Take your leg back until the heel is close to the bottom, keeping the knees together. Hold for 8-10 seconds. Repeat with the other leg. This stretches the quadricep muscles on the front of the thigh.

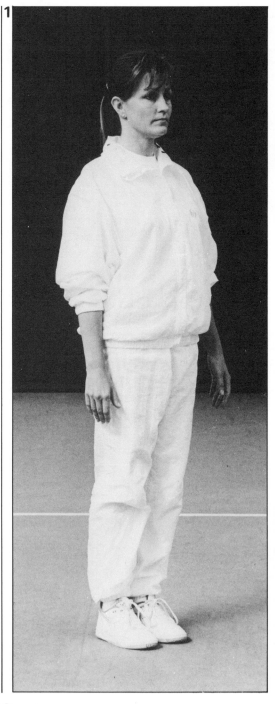

Note: All the exercises included in this warming-up section are called 'active' stretches with the player carrying out the exercise himself. Sometimes there is a case for doing 'passive' stretches, in which a second person is involved in manipulating the limbs. This is more likely when the player has been injured, and needs the help of a qualified physiotherapist or trainer to assist his rehabilitation.

2

3

Calf stretch

1 Stand with legs 'staggered' – one foot in front of the other, and shoulder-width apart. Ensure that both feet are pointing forwards, with the rear heel flat on the floor.

2 Bend the front leg, supporting the body weight on the thigh, and keeping the rear leg straight, the heel down. Hold for 10 seconds. Repeat, reversing the leg positions. This stretches the calf muscles and achilles tendons.

CHAPTER TWO

FITNESS AND STAMINA

What is fitness? How is it measured? True fitness for a tennis player encompasses many different things, but the bottom line is that fitness is a condition in which the muscles of the body have the maximum capability to store and burn fuel. The simple way to measure fitness is to find out how long it takes for the pulse rate to return to normal after exercise.

Both statements are a simplification, but in lay-man's terms, improving fitness means developing the capacity of the muscles to function, and developing the ability of the cardiovascular system to deliver oxygen to the muscles.

Fatigue is caused by a lack of fuel being supplied to the muscles, and by an accumulation of lactic acid, due to a shortage of oxygen. The idea in training is to place an over-load on the cardiovascular system.

Stamina is the foundation of fitness, and can be developed in a variety of ways: through running, swimming, cycling or circuit training. But before examining some different routines, there are a few basic points to mention.

Measuring your fitness level

The first thing to do is to discover your basic fitness level. Put two or three fingers across the inside of the opposite wrist, and count the pulse beats over a 60-second period. That will give you your 'resting' pulse rate. It is likely to be between 50 and 90, depending on age and lifestyle.

Follow up by doing three minutes of quite strenuous exercise like running up and down the stairs, or doing continuous step-ups on and off a low bench. Now take the pulse rate again. It should not be much more than half as much again. For example, if your resting pulse rate is 70, the rate after three minutes' activity should not be much more than 105.

Now rest and try to establish how long it takes for your pulse to return to normal. For the average person it should take about two minutes. The fitter you are, the quicker your recovery time.

If it takes more than three minutes, you are quite unfit, and need to build up slowly. In fact, anybody who is unused to regular exercise should take things very gradually, starting with a few minutes of exercises every day, before moving on to anything more strenuous.

General rules for training

Once you get into a fitness programme, make sure that you wear comfortable, loose-fitting clothes. And take the trouble to get good running shoes. Choose shoes that have plenty of cushioning in the soles. Many tennis players take extra care by having sorbothane inserts individually shaped for their shoes, to help guard against injuries. I always like to have plenty of room in my tennis shoes, so that I can wear two pairs of socks for extra comfort.

Try to avoid doing too much road running. Always run on grass – round the park or cross-country, for instance – rather than on pavements or roads. Injuries like shin-splints, or even stress fractures, can

develop from too much pounding of hard surfaces.

The best training I ever did was as a member of the Barrett Boys scheme, run by the LTA under the leadership of John Barrett. We lodged at the YMCA in Wimbledon, London, and ran seven to eight miles every morning before breakfast around Wimbledon Common. It was a 'timed' run, and we would follow-up with a schedule of press-ups, sit-ups and knee jumps. As a result of that training, we built up stamina and endurance, and we knew we were not going to get tired in a long match.

I'm not suggesting that the average club player should follow that sort of regime. But a three to four mile run, three days a week, would provide an excellent basis for general fitness. However, if you are unfit, take care to build up slowly and gradually, increasing the distance and the pace as you get fitter and stronger.

Swimming is a good alternative to running for achieving stamina. Half an hour of disciplined lengths of a full-sized or 33 metre pool is ideal for developing lung capacity. For added strength, try pulling yourself out of the pool using the arms only, after every length!

Variety is always a good thing in your training, particularly in stamina work, to help beat boredom and to help protect against injury. Swimming is obviously ideal for avoiding injuries from vibration. Cycling, too, has its advantages. For strengthening the legs, cycling is better in

Opposite: Boris Becker has a winning combination of strength, stamina, speed and agility. His high level of fitness has made him one of the top fast-court players in the world.

some ways than running. The action of pedalling is smooth and rhythmic, avoiding the pounding that legs can take on long runs. However, you don't have to go outside on the roads to cycle; the kind of exercise bikes found in health clubs are excellent for general fitness work.

If you are doing serious stamina work, one way to increase the value of your run, without spending more time at it, is to run with a pack on your back. An extra 4.5 kg/10 lb of weight to carry makes a big difference. When I was doing the morning run with the Barrett Boys, I wore heavy Army boots, and also had 1 kg/2 lb weights strapped around my ankles to increase the work load. In fact, I used to play most of my practice sets wearing the weights. Psychologically that had an impact. When I played a match without the weights, I used to feel that much sharper and faster.

There was no such thing as a 'Walkman' in those days. But nowadays many players train with a personal stereo. It helps to take the drudgery out of training. I recall training with Arsenal Football Club one year, when I was recovering from a cartilage operation, and they did all their gym work to music. It helps to get a rhythm going, as well as making the hard work less boring.

Tennis is a sport that requires both pace and stamina. It combines the 100 metres with the 10,000 metres. You can introduce this element into training. One-pace running has only a certain value. More valuable is what is called 'interval' running. You introduce into a long-distance run, shorter bursts of speed over distances that can vary from 50 to 100 metres. Some players have a totally structured session in which they will run perhaps 20 bursts of 50-metre sprints, with a 50 or 100-metre recovery period in between, which is done at a jog. That way they are covering up to 3000 metres, half of it at speed. It is the kind of routine that helps to develop stamina, but also works on developing your sprinting speed at the same time.

Circuit training

Circuit training is an excellent way to develop stamina, particularly if you have the use of a gymnasium. The members of the Slater Boys squad that we train at the David Lloyd clubs, regularly do circuit training with a routine that is carefully designed not to overload young bodies.

But it is not necessary to have top-class facilities to be able to do circuit training. You can devise a very worthwhile range of exercises without using any equipment at all. The basic idea of a circuit is to perform a number of different exercises in turn, using all the different muscle groups. The aim should be to design the routine so that the same muscles are not stressed in consecutive exercises.

The beauty of it is that you can increase the intensity of the work merely by adding more repetitions, or cutting down the recovery time between circuits. And in circumstances where you have access to equipment, such as in a gym, obviously you can use heavier weights.

Here is a circuit-training routine that can be done at home without the need for any equipment at all, other than a low bench or perhaps a large block of wood.

Bench steps

Step on and off the bench, concentrating on raising the knees high, and keeping the back straight. If you don't have a bench, you can just do a high-stepping routine on the spot. Try to maintain a good rhythm,

and get the thighs up to a horizontal position. Start with 20 seconds of exercise and increase them gradually to 30 seconds as you get fitter. This exercise works on the quads and gluttal muscles.

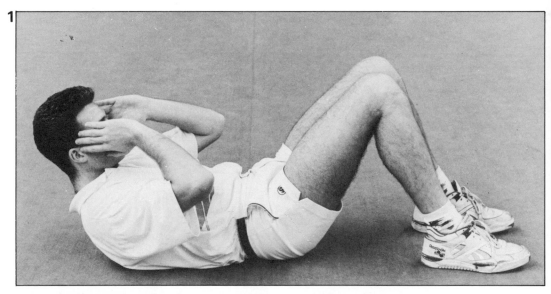

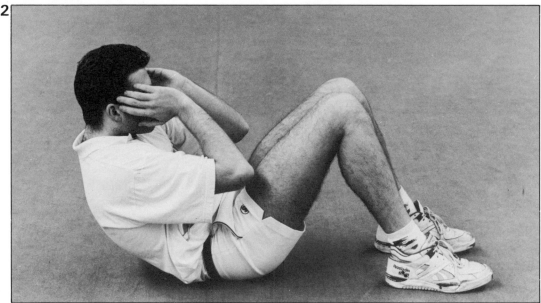

Sit-ups

1 Lie on your back, hands beside the head, and knees bent.

2 Curl up and touch the thighs with the elbows. Do as many repetitions as you can in 20-30 seconds, avoiding jerking or pulling on the head. Ensure that the lower back stays in contact with the floor at all times.

Squat thrusts

1 Start from a 'press-up' position, with your weight on the hands and toes, and the back straight.
2 Then 'jump' both feet forward into a crouching position, making sure that the knees are level with the arms.
3 Jump back to the start position, and repeat continuously for 20-30 seconds. This exercise works on the quads and hamstrings.

Swallows

1 Lie on the stomach, arms at the sides.
2 Then raise the head and shoulders and legs off the floor, arching the back. Hold for a few seconds, and lower. Do 20-30 seconds' controlled movements. Do not arch too far. It is not good to hyper-extend.

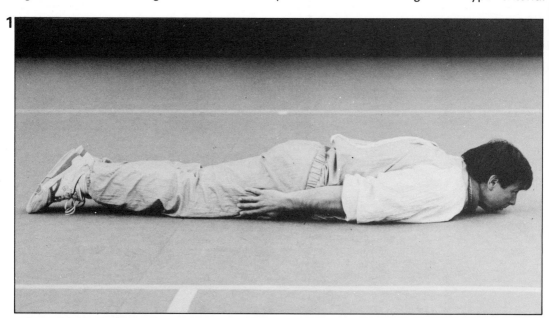

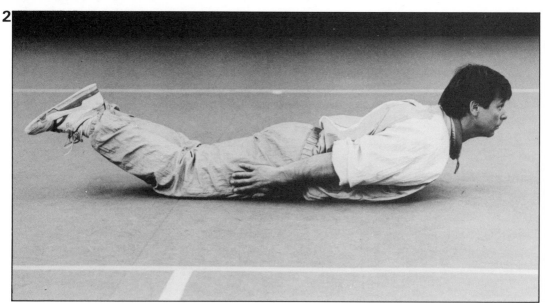

Plyometric knee-jumps

1 Stand up, nice and relaxed, arms folded at shoulder height.

2 Bend both your knees until you are in a half squatting position.

3 Then spring up, achieving as much height as possible, minimizing momentum by keeping the arms still. Do 20-30 seconds' repetitions.

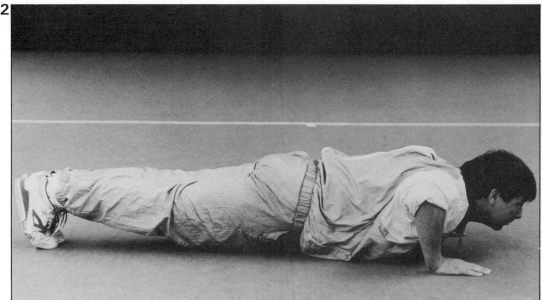

Press-ups

1 Keeping the body straight, lie down with the body weight supported by the arms and toes. Start with the arms straight, hands on the ground, level with the shoulders. **2** Bend the arms to lower the chest to the ground, then push back up, keeping the

body straight. Again, do 20-30 seconds' repetitions. This exercise works the pectoral, deltoid and tricep muscles.

Variation: 1 & 2 Women should keep their knees on the ground so that the pivot point is further up the body and there is less weight for them to push up.

Stride jumps

1 Stand astride the low bench or block of wood.

2 Jump with both feet simultaneously on to the bench.

3 Then immediately jump off the bench. Jump on and off in this way for 20-30 seconds. This exercise works the quadriceps and calf muscles.

When you first start doing circuit-training, you can either do each exercise for a specific period – say, 20 or 30 seconds – and count how many repetitions you can manage in that time, or you can select a number of repetitions to do for each exercise. The slight drawback there is that some exercises take longer to complete, or are more demanding than others.

The preferred method is to do each exercise for the same amount of time. Then your target is to try to increase the number of repetitions within that period. As you get fitter, you can also increase the number of circuits you perform; and cut down on the recovery time between each circuit.

SPEED AND FLEXIBILITY

When Michael Chang won the French Open men's singles in 1989, it was very interesting to analyse how he did it. He was very small. He lacked natural power of stroke. He didn't have a big serve. He rarely went to the net. His actual tennis game didn't compare with the big names like Lendl, Edberg or Becker. Yet he won it, and nobody could say that he did not deserve his triumph.

How did he do it? The answer is that Chang won the French Open by virtue, almost entirely, of his sheer speed, mobility, and fitness. On a slow surface, like the clay courts in Paris, opponents found it almost impossible to put the ball away against Chang. His retrieving from the baseline was fantastic. That skill is based on his speed around the court. It is an asset derived from the tremendous power in his legs. Chang has massive strength in his legs, built up by years of dedicated training.

Strong legs do not just develop sheer speed. Pace alone is not enough. The strength is required for the constant stopping and starting; the pushing off from one leg; the twisting and turning; and the jumping.

Take away Michael Chang's speed, and he has nothing, in terms of world-class tennis. But his pace and mobility still make him a world-class performer on slow surfaces.

Speed, in tennis, is linked to flexibility and agility. There is no call to run 100 yards when you are playing tennis. The longest distance you can run on court is about 20 yards. The average movement is probably between 5 and 10 yards.

As you are bending down to most ground shots you have to learn to sprint 'low' – to keep down as you move, to save vital split seconds. Tennis players are very rarely fully upright when moving to the ball. You therefore need to train for that type of movement. Longer sprints can be used to build up basic pace, but don't neglect the bending and twisting element.

In developing speed around the court, the best training exercises involve using the court itself for sprint drills. The two best routines are the Line Exercise and the Ball Shuttle Run.

Opposite: Michael Chang lacks the height and power of many top professionals, but he makes up for this with his speed, agility and a high level of fitness. He is a great exponent of the benefits to be derived from practice and training and has worked hard to develop a scientific approach to his game and to achieve his form at the apex of international tennis.

Line exercise

1 Start from the 'T' junction at the centre of the court. Face the net.
2 Sidestep to the outside line.
3 Sprint to the net.
4 Sidestep across to the opposite sideline.
5 Run backwards to the baseline.
6 Sidestep across the court to the opposite sideline.
7 Sprint up to the net.
8 Sidestep to the centre.
9 And run backwards to finish at the 'T' junction.

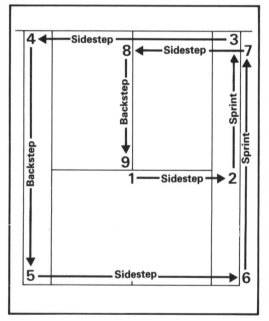

That one routine covers all the movements you need in the game. Sideways, back-pedalling, turning and forward sprinting. Try to use short, pitter-patter steps. You don't see tennis players, generally speaking, taking large strides around the court. Small steps make it much easier to get into the perfect position for striking the ball effectively.

Time yourself on the first run, and then keep trying to improve on your time. Repeat the exercise 5-6 times in each training session, allowing about 30 seconds rest between each run.

Ball shuttle run

1 Take four balls with you on court. Put one ball on the inside tramline, one ball on the centre service line, one ball on the far tramline, and the last ball on the far sideline. Each ball should be the same distance from the net.
2 Start the drill from the sideline. Take a step or two, bend and pick up the first ball.
3 Turn and put it down where you started from.
4 Sprint to the centre line, pick up the ball, and place it with the first.
5 Collect all four balls as quickly as possible, in the same manner.

A good tip is to take a small box onto the court. When you retrieve each ball, and

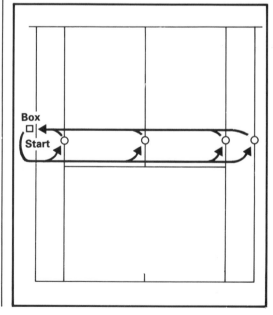

return to the sideline, make sure you put the ball in the box. Doing that just increases the demands on hand/eye co-ordination, putting more emphasis on control in the exercise.

This is also a drill that reproduces the stop-and-start movements, the bending and turning and the sprinting you need in a game. Again, time your first run, and try to keep improving it.

The photograph above shows how the balls are positioned on the court for the Ball Shuttle Run drill as described on the opposite page.

Training with a partner

It's always good to train with a partner, so that you can introduce an element of competition into the drills. Racing against somebody else on the other side of the net helps you push yourself that much harder.

Of course, there are variations of both drills. There are a number of different versions of the Line Exercise. One of the best is the one I call the 'Figure of eight'.

Figure of eight line drill

1 Start the exercise on the 'T' junction at the centre of the court. Sprint diagonally up to the net, and touch the left-hand net-post.
2 Sideways-step across court, and touch the right-hand net-post.
3 Run backwards diagonally across to the left-hand baseline corner.
4 Sidestep across to the right-hand corner.
5 Finish by sprinting diagonally back to the centre.

Another good variation on this exercise introduces 'shadow play' into the routine. This involves playing imaginary shots as part of the drill.

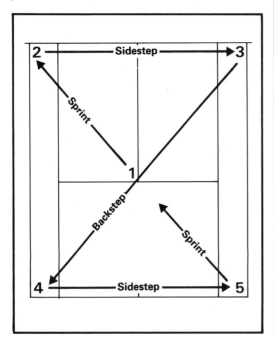

Shadow drill

1 Start on the centre of the baseline. Sprint up to the net.
2 Sidestep across to the right-hand tramline, and 'Shadow play' a forehand volley
3 Sidestep back across the net to the left tramline, and play a backhand volley.
4 Backstep to the baseline, and shadow a backhand drive.
5 Sidestep across to the forehand corner, and stroke a forehand drive.
6 Finish with a sidestep to the middle.

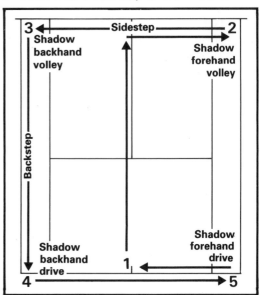

This drill has the virtue of introducing some of the strokes into a fitness exercise. Try to 'shadow' the shots with a perfect technique, getting the footwork and body positions right.

There are a similar number of variations of the Ball Shuttle Run. When working more on basic fitness and speed, rather than mobility, you can line up several balls on the far sideline, and do the full width of the court on each run. Or you can do the original shuttle routine, but having picked up each ball, run backwards to the sideline to place it in the box.

A little refinement is to use a racket instead of a box. The player has to put the balls on the racket face. Having collected all four balls, the player has to pick up the racket from the ground and, keeping the balls on the strings, run across the court, and back. If any balls are dropped, he has to repeat the whole drill.

All these drills should be timed, so that you have a target time to try to better.

Ball roll

1 One player stands on the 'T' junction, with a supply of balls. The second player stands at the centre of the baseline.

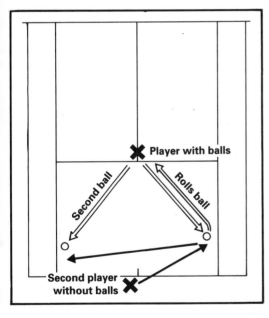

2 The first player rolls a ball towards the corner of the court.

3 The second player darts forward, and across, to intercept, fields the ball, and rolls it back to the centre. By this time, the second ball is on its way to the opposite

corner. Keep the exercise going from side to side for 60 seconds. Then change roles.

Once again, the drill involves all the elements of movement you need in a game – sprinting, stopping, bending, turning, pushing-off, plus the hand-eye co-ordination of stopping and rolling back the balls.

All the time you are training, the more types of movement, twisting and turning that you can introduce to all the drills described here, the better.

Squad training

When you have a squad situation, with five or six players training together, you can introduce relay-races and other variations. One enjoyable routine is called the Fox and hounds.

Fox and hounds

1 Mark off one half of one end of the court, i.e., use the back half of a court from the service line to the baseline.

2 Line the players up at one corner.

3 One player will be the fox. He starts off the drill, sprinting round the rectangle.

4 When he is halfway round, the first hound starts, with the aim of trying to catch the fox. If he has failed to catch the fox after one full circuit (for the hound), he sends the second hound.

5 If he has failed to catch up after one lap, he in turn releases the next hound. The fox, meanwhile, just keeps running round, trying to keep ahead. Eventually one of the hounds will catch the fox. Count the laps it takes to catch the fox. After a few minutes' breather, start the drill again, with a different fox. Keep repeating the drill until every player has had a turn as the fox. The winner will be the fox who completes most laps before being caught.

CHAPTER FOUR

STRENGTH TRAINING

Tennis players need to be strong, and they have to have strength in specific muscles. But it is strength without bulk that is needed and it is a handicap to be muscle-bound. Building strength for playing tennis does not mean developing a weightlifter's physique; that would be counter-productive. Strength allied with mobility is the key to playing tennis well.

So in all the different weight-training exercises I recommend, the emphasis is on light weights with fast repetitions, rather than on lifting heavy weights. The aim is to develop 'fast' muscle for explosive power.

A few words of warning also: it is important while doing strength training not to overbalance the body. For example, if you are trying to build up the shoulder muscles, make sure that you do not just work on the racket arm. If you build up the muscles on one side only, you risk serious injury and the spine may become pulled out of line. Always balance up. Work equally hard on both sides, or you are asking for trouble. Also, most muscles come in pairs: one muscle flexes a joint, whereas its partner straightens it. It is best to exercise both muscles in a pair. Certainly it is unwise to build up one muscle and neglect its pair.

If you are using weights to train with, it is best to underestimate the 'load' with which you should work. If you then find the exercise easy, you can always increase the amount of weight. Remember, the amount of weights you use should allow quick, comfortable repetitions of each exercise, unless you are specifically trying to build bulk using heavier weights.

If you have access to a good gymna-sium, it is easy to get advice and help with weight training. And modern weight machines make it easy to 'identify' specific muscles to work on. But you can still do good weight training at home with just a couple of dumbbells and a barbell.

It is hard to think of a sport that uses a greater range of muscles than tennis. The different strokes and movements require good muscle tone throughout the body. At first sight, you might think only the arms and shoulders are important for wielding a racket. But then consider the stress placed on the stomach and back muscles during the service – Stefan Edberg's for instance. And note the tremendous power that is generated from Boris Becker's knee bend on the serve.

All the main muscle groups in the body come into play in tennis and the range of exercises you perform has to reflect this. Strengthening the muscles does three things:
● It helps to develop greater power of shot;
● It also helps to master techniques, because skills can be restricted if the player lacks the basic strength to perform a certain stroke;
● Development of muscles and ligaments helps to protect joints from injury.

When doing any of the exercises, try to develop a rhythmic breathing pattern, aiming to breathe in on the effort of lifting.

Free weight exercises

This is a series of exercises you can do with the use of dumbbells and a barbell, which cover all the main muscle groups. Start off with 10 repetitions of each, and build up.

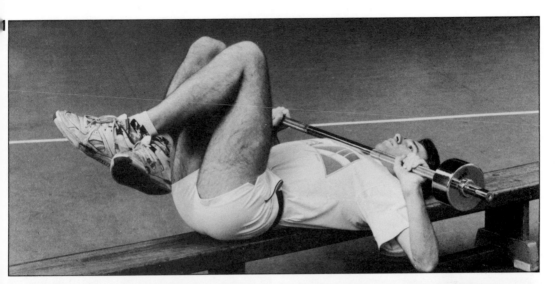

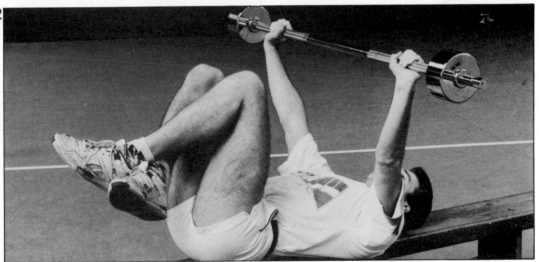

The chest press

This exercise will develop the chest, the front shoulder muscles, and those on the back of the upper arm.

1 Lie on your back, preferably on a long bench with your feet on the bench, ensuring your lower back is flat, arms bent, holding a barbell vertically.

2 Push up to straighten the arms, and then lower gently.

Note: You can put extra weights on to increase the loading. If you do fit extra weights on to the bar, make sure that the collars are properly secured before starting the exercise. If preferred, you can used dumbbells. This exercise works the pectorals, deltoids and triceps.

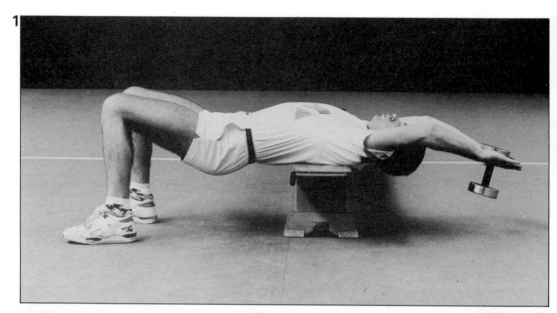

The straight arm pull-over

1 Lie on your back, with the barbell or dumbbells held at arms' length behind the head.

2 Pull the bar slowly up until your arms are vertical above your head. Then return to the starting position.

This exercise works on the chest, the shoulders, and the lower back muscles and helps to expand the rib cage.

The press behind the neck

1 Stand with feet apart, and the bar resting behind the neck.

2 Push the bar up until the arms are straight and extended above the head

This is another good exercise for developing the shoulder muscles, which are so vital for serving and overhead shots.

Front squats

1 Stand straight, feet apart, the bar resting across the chest.
2 Keeping the back perfectly straight, now

lower the body into the squat position.
3 Push back up to a standing position.
This is a good exercise for strengthening the front thigh muscles – the kind of work Michael Chang must have done for hours to develop the power in his legs.

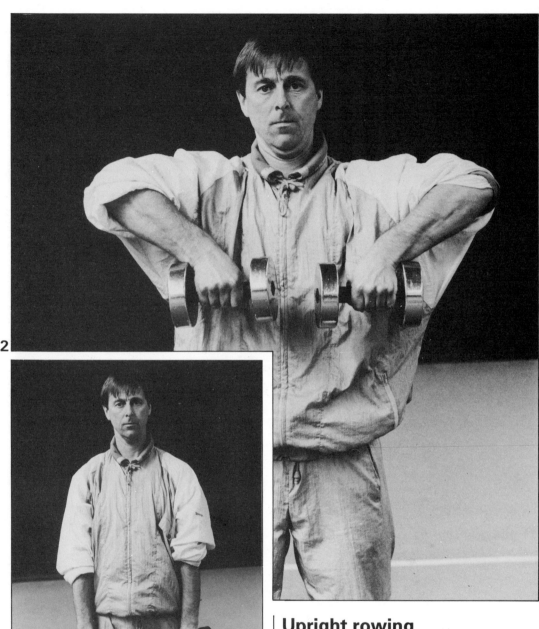

2

1

Upright rowing

This is an exercise for developing the upper back muscles, and the forearms and shoulders. It can be done with a single barbell, or with two dumbbells.

1 Stand up straight, and hold the bar or the dumbbells at arms' length, resting against the thighs. The knuckles should be to the front.

2 & 3 Pull the bar or the dumbbells up to chin height, keeping the wrists facing forwards – in other words, don't allow the hands to come underneath the bar.

1

2

Lunges *Opposite and below*

This is an exercise that develops strength and flexibility in the legs, especially the quads. Good mobility of the knee joints is vital in tennis for playing low ground shots and volleys.

1 Start the exercise with the bar held resting on the shoulders. Position one foot well out in front, the other foot well to the rear. The heel of the back foot should be raised.

2 Now lower the body by bending the legs from the knees. Push down until the front knee is at right angles but not beyond the foot. Straighten up, and repeat the exercise, reversing the position of the feet.

Variation: You can also do this exercise with dumbbells as shown below. Do exactly the same as outlined for the lunge with barbell as shown opposite.

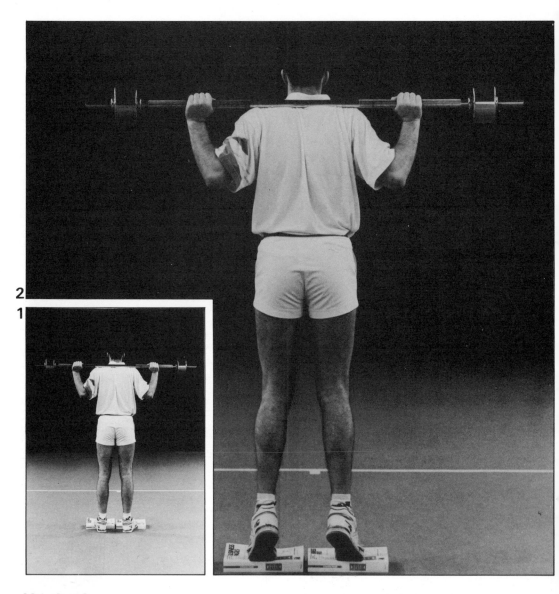

Heel raise

1 Place two hard-backed books, a telephone directory or similar objects about 2.5-4 cm/1-1½ in thick, on the floor. Position the barbell across the back of the shoulders. Now step onto the books, with your toes positioned on the books, but with the heels still resting on the floor.

2 Rise up as high as possible on the toes, to work the achilles tendons and calf muscles. For added emphasis, squeeze the calf muscles in the top position for 2-3 seconds.

3 Lower the heels to the floor.

Curls

This exercise will strengthen the arms, back and stomach muscles.

1 Stand up straight, holding the dumbbells, at arms' length.

2 Holding the dumbbells with an undergrip and keeping elbows tucked into the body, pull one dumbbell up to the chest, using only the arm. Make sure the back stays straight and the head keeps still.

3 Lower the arm slowly and raise the other arm. You can also use a barbell for this exercise.

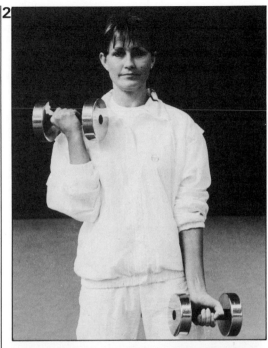

If you have access to a well-equipped gymnasium, all these exercises, and many more, can be duplicated on modern machines. And there is likely to be a qualified instructor to help advise on the correct 'loading' and techniques. I will therefore not try to go into any detail on the use of multi-gyms or similar equipment. It is sufficient to say that whatever equipment you use, you need a good range of exercises to develop strength and mobility at tennis. As I have said before, the service on its own requires power in the legs, back, stomach, shoulders and wrists. That doesn't leave much else!

Naturally the better the facilities at your disposal for training, the better. However, you can build up strength without specialized weight machines, or even without a bar and dumbbells. You just have to do the exercises and improvise on new ways of increasing the stress. Muscular power is developed by maximum contraction of the muscle, followed by explosive extension. Strength can only be developed by creating 'resistance' for the muscles.

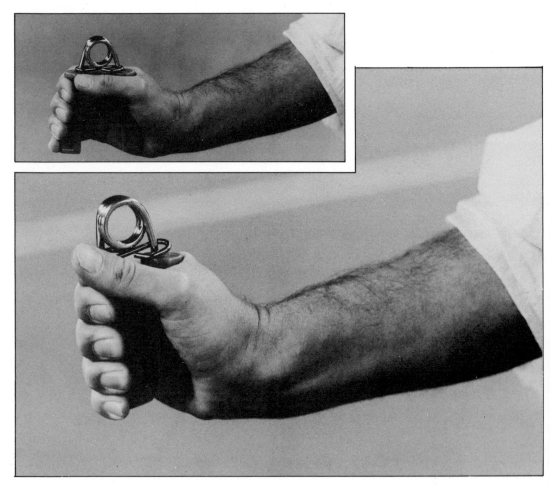

That resistance does not have to be a purpose-built machine or weight; it can be any balanced object that can be easily handled.

Developing wrist and arm strength

A good thick book can be used to help strengthen the wrists and forearms. Hold the book – any heavy volume will do – in the hand. Rest the forearm on the edge of a table, with the palm of the hand over the edge. Use the wrist to lower and raise the book through the full range of movement. Repeat the exercise with the palm up, raising and lowering the book as far as it will go.

Many tennis players carry a squash ball around with them – not to play squash but to strengthen the wrist and fingers. It's something they can do at any time of the day – while watching television or on an aeroplane, or at any spare moment. The idea is to squeeze the squash ball, continually opening and closing the fingers. The exercise can be performed, in fact, without a ball. If you stretch the fingers wide, and then clench into a very tight fist, and hold for a few seconds, you get the same value as you would from squeezing a ball. Stretch and clench the fist repeatedly until you can do 100 repetitions without a break.

Another good routine for developing the wrists and arms makes use of an old racket handle, or perhaps a piece of broom handle. Attach a weight, or heavy object, to the handle, on the end of a piece of thin rope about 1 m/3 ft long. Grip the handle on either side of the rope, and 'wind' up the weight by turning with one hand at a time. Lower the weight by using the other hand to turn the handle. Alternate the hands in raising and lowering the weight.

Increasing the stress in exercises

Exercises like press-ups and sit-ups can also be made tougher to put more loading on to the muscles. To increase the stress on **press-ups**, merely raise the feet. Instead of having the feet resting on the floor, position them on the bottom step of the stairs, for example. The second step up will increase the pressure.

To strengthen the **stomach muscles**, lie on your back, and 'anchor' the feet, bringing your heels in close to your bottom. You may cross your arms across your chest if wished, but if you do so, you must perform the exercise more slowly. Pull the body up into a sitting position.

The **quadriceps** – the front muscles of the thigh – are very important for tennis players. They not only provide power for jumping, stopping and starting, and sprinting; but they also play an important part in supporting the knee joint. Twisting and turning, and bending and stretching, place a big strain on the knees. The stronger the 'quads' are, the better for you and your game. They are easy to exercise while sitting at home in front of the television. Footballers recovering from cartilage operations spend hours building up the muscles on the front of the thighs. They wear special iron 'boots' and sit on a chair, continually raising the foot until the leg is straight. When recovering from my own cartilage operation, I tied weights around my ankle, and did the same leg raising and lowering exercises.

Even without weights, it is a useful exercise, because the knee is such a vital joint for a tennis player. There has to be full flexibility of the knee joint to be able to get down to low balls, particularly low volleys.

CHAPTER FIVE

ON-COURT DRILLS

Jimmy Connors was one of the fittest players I ever came across in my career, and certainly the toughest match player. He ran down every ball, and never gave in until the last point had been won or lost. Yet Jimmy probably spent less time on training than any of the other modern 'greats'. Jimbo always believed that the best place to train for tennis was on the tennis court. He wasn't one for gym work, or long-distance runs. He just slogged through hour after hour of concentrated practice on court.

Although I do believe that training is an essential part of fitness for most tennis players, there's no question that the more time you can spend on court, hitting balls the better. There are plenty of good practice drills you can do, that combine speed and stamina work with improvement of technique. The important thing is to practise properly, with a real sense of purpose and, above all, concentration.

The best drills involve some form of competitive element, either against someone else, or in striving to achieve targets. Concentrating hard to try to hit targets on the court, while also working physically hard, is mentally very tiring, and good training for match play.

Most good practice drills are also very simple to set up, requiring just one, or two other players to work with. Remember to warm up properly before you go into a strenuous routine.

Two simple drills used by many top players in practice are as follows:

Cross-court and down the line

1 Working with a partner, you decide before starting that one player (A) will hit every ball across court, while the other (B) will hit every ball down the line.

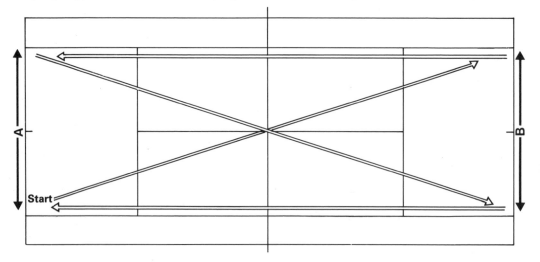

2 Player A starts the rally, hitting a forehand across court.

3 Player B has to respond by hitting a forehand down the line.

4 Player A is then required to hit a backhand cross-court, making Player B hit a backhand down the line. The routine can then start all over again. The aim is to keep the ball going for as long as possible. The idea in practice – early on certainly – is to keep the ball in court.

Don't try to hit winners to start with; instead, try to keep the ball deep when hitting down the line, and into the corners when hitting cross-court. This is a very good drill for technique and fitness. Both players are covering a lot of ground, although the player having to return down the line has to cover more ground in reaching the cross-court shots. Obviously the players reverse the roles after a few minutes.

Cross-court/down the line variation

1 When a player is keen to work on one particular ground shot, the professionals use a variation of the previous drill. One player will stay in one corner of the court, to hit every shot with either forehand or backhand (depending on which corner). He will alternate between cross-court or down the line shots, while his practice partner has to hit forehands and backhands back to the same corner.

2 If player A wants to work on his forehand, he starts off hitting a cross-court forehand.

3 Player B replies with a cross-court forehand.

4 Player A strikes the next forehand down the line and player B has to return a backhand down the line and so on. This is a

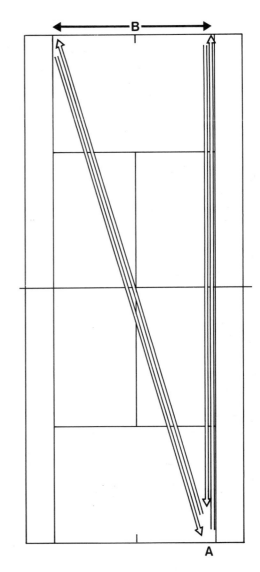

routine I have watched André Agassi and Monica Seles following for hours at the Nick Bolletièri School.

And that is another point: Agassi has the best forehand in the world. That does not mean that he doesn't have to practise it! It is the best – because he spends hours working on it.

Feeding from the net drill

One of the best practice drills, which is also extremely physically and mentally tiring, involves one player 'feeding' from the net by hand.

1 Player A stands on or just behind the baseline. His partner has a supply of balls. The aim of the drill is for the hitter to play every ball with the same shot, no matter where the ball is thrown. If the 'feeder' nominates forehand, Player A has to use the forehand on every shot; if the ball is placed into the backhand corner, he has to run round his backhand, and still play a forehand stroke.

2 The player at the net will vary the 'feed', placing one ball into the forehand corner, the next into the centre, followed by one into the backhand corner, and so on. It is a wonderful drill for improving footwork and speed, as well as stamina. It can be made tougher, and more mentally demanding, if the player has to aim every shot at a particular area of the court. Not only has he to hit every ball with the same shot, but into the same target area. It's tough!

Controlled drills

Putting a 'control' on a practice routine adds to the value, by forcing greater concentration. Going back to Agassi, I have seen him working on court at Bolletièri's in various controlled drills.

One is where he is faced by two 'feeders' at the net, supplying a constant stream of balls. He has to make every return without

Opposite: Jimmy Connors believed in doing most of his training and practise on the tennis court itself. Right: Monica Seles practices the cross-court and down the line drill to sharpen up her performance in matches.

going behind the baseline. He is not allowed to step back, but has to take every ball inside the baseline, going forward. It is a pressure routine that teaches an aggressive, early-ball approach. Standing in close also helps to cut down the recovery time between shots, and therefore is physically demanding.

For practising return of service, Agassi will face players serving at him at full pace, but from well inside the court, even from the other service line. He has to return the serve from inside the baseline. This is a type of practice used to help players work on service returns, by stopping them taking too big a backswing.

'Two-on-one' drills are a favourite form of practice with most top players, because of the added intensity. Two players together at the net can put a baseliner under much more pressure than a single practice partner can do.

Volleying drills

These are particularly good in a two-on-one situation; the single player can be put under constant pressure, helping to develop reaction speed. One 'control' that top players will use in a volleying drill is that each player should stay inside the service line. Any player stepping back beyond the service line loses the point in a competitive drill; that doesn't sound very tough, but we are talking about really hard, punched volleys, driven at the body.

When I was in the Barrett Boys squad, we used to do the volleying drill without a shirt on, and try to hit each other with the ball. Believe me, it hurt! But it taught us to develop lightning reflexes, and good racket skills in defending the body.

Stamina-building drills

Another practice drill that develops pace and stamina, and also really stretches the joints, involves one player acting as a feeder at the net, with a supply of balls.

1 The feeder stands close to the net, and just drops a ball gently a yard or so over the net to one side of the court.

2 The volleyer starts two or three yards away from the net. As the ball is dropped over the net, he has to move forwards, and bend low to play a controlled volley.

3 As he makes contact, the feeder releases another ball to the other side; the volleyer has to get across and play another volley and immediately move back across for the next shot.

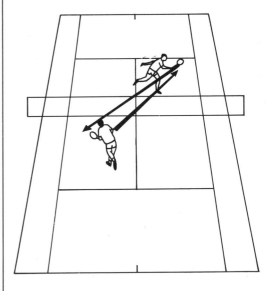

A few minutes of constant bending and stretching, and turning back across the court, are very demanding, and having to play controlled shots off a soft ball, with no pace, is an added pressure. It is particularly good practice for doubles play.

Targets on the court

Placing targets on the court is another way of increasing the intensity of practice. Again, it is something that the very best players do. Putting a ball can, or box, a couple of feet inside the baseline, and the same distance from the sideline, helps a player to focus on the target at which he is aiming. If you spend 30 minutes a day aiming at a particular target, it gets imprinted on the brain. When you get into a rally in a match, it seems natural to be still aiming for a target.

In practice, count the number of times you hit the target. Try to improve on it every time. Try to beat your practice partner's score. It is surprising how much easier it is to direct your shots, when you have a specific target.

Smash and touch the net drills

This is a very popular stamina-building routine.

1 Player A begins the routine, standing midway between the net and the service line.

2 The feeder has a bucket of balls; he hits a lob of three-quarter length over Player A.

3 Player A has to move back and hit the smash; then run up to touch the net with his racket, and backpedal for the next smash. Count only the smashes that go into court, and complete 10 repetitions of the drill. As you get fitter, progress to 15, then 20 and up to 25.

A variation of the routine is to hit alternate smash and volley; the feeder will lob one ball for the smash, and feed the next ball short and low. The player has to make the volley, and not allow the ball to bounce.

These are physically demanding drills that develop stamina as well as technique.

Drills to keep the ball in court

Practice drills are always most effective when there is a reward for accuracy – or a punishment for errors. In other words, even when doing drills for fitness, there should be some sort of emphasis on keeping the ball in court. For instance, when the boys in the Slater Foundation squad are practising ground shots, they have to reach a target of 100 shots correctly hit while under pressure from two feeders. But every mistake means they lose five from their score. That target of 100 can seem a long way distant if they make a lot of errors! But they have to keep going without a break until they reach the target.

Some coaches will make pupils do 10 press-ups, or something similar, every time they make an unforced error. It may sound brutal, but tournament tennis is tough. Simple mistakes have to be eliminated.

There is no point in being fit and strong and quick as lightning, if you cannot keep the ball in the court. That is why it is best to introduce a competitive element into all practice routines.

Tramline drill

Two players rally from the baseline, and have to hit every ball within the tramlines. Obviously, one player usually hits forehands, and the other will hit backhands but it is not essential. A good control is to require both players to hit forehands, or to alternate backhands and forehands, and so on. The real test is to keep the ball inside the lines. After all, the tramlines are only 1.37 metres/4½ feet wide.

CHAPTER SIX

MENTAL FITNESS

The best thing that ever happened to me – as far as my tennis career is concerned – was being sent on an Outward Bound Course, while I was part of the Barrett Boys scheme. It was terrific. I loved it, and went back again. The Outward Bound course taught me so much about the mental approach to life and problem solving and this helped me in my tennis career, too.

Tennis is at least 50 per cent in the mind – possibly more. Having great technique and athleticism is just not enough to be a winner and a great player. To be a winner, you need: confidence; concentration; control; determination; courage; and ambition. It all comes under the umbrella of mental fitness. The mental approach to the game has to be right.

Proof of this is to be found everywhere at tennis tournaments at every level of the game, from tiny tots to Grand Slam championships, You only need to go to the practice courts to find it.

Watching two players practising at Wimbledon, for example, if they were just 'hitting' and not playing points, it would be hard for the average person to judge who was the better player. They would both be fit and strong, quick and agile; they would both have powerful shots, struck with excellent technique; they would both be able to hit every shot in the book – ground shots with topspin or slice (or hit flat), crisp volleys, inch-perfect lobs, and a full range of different serves. They would look absolutely evenly matched. But it is quite likely that one of the two players would beat the other in a match without hardly breaking sweat.

The reason is to be found in the mind. The best players can produce their best shots when they have to do so – under pressure. The others can't. It is almost as simple as that. For some reason it seems to happen to British players more than most. In Britain, we produce plenty of very talented players, with all the necessary physical qualities. But under pressure, in the heat of a match, they cannot produce it.

It is exactly the same at club level. Some players look like world-beaters in the knock-up; but once a match starts – or even just a friendly set – they cannot get the ball over the net.

All club players who play competitively know the meaning of the term 'elbow'. It is the condition that seems to lock your arm solid, or drain it of all strength, just as you are serving for the match, or facing a match point.

Champions also know the feeling. They have been through it all before, and learned how to cope. Everybody gets nerves, but the best players know how to control them. There are various mental tricks of the trade to overcome nerves, and to help with concentration, self-control, confidence and attitude.

I think it is important for players to know what type of person they are under pres-

Opposite: Throughout his career at the top of international tennis, Bjorn Borg always thought positively on court. This enabled him not only to overcome his injuries but also to play magnificently under pressure.

sure; how they react to stress and adversity. Attending the Outward Bound course taught me a lot about myself. It was a great character-builder. On Outward Bound courses you need discipline; you face situations you would not normally face; have to solve problems you have never been set before . . . like pitching a tent blindfolded, inside a certain time, or building a bivouac to sleep in, while dumped in the middle of a forest in freezing temperatures, or rock-climbing on a sheer face, where you in turn hold the life of your colleague in your hands, and then have to let someone else hold your life in his, or learning to life-save from a cutter in the freezing waters of the North Sea.

They are all situations where you have to think calmly and positively, keep your nerve, and act with control. It can be like that in a tennis match. It may not be a matter of life and death on court, but winners treat it as such.

Sport is a reflection of life. A player reacts under pressure on court the same way as he reacts to stress in a personal relationship, or in a crisis at work. The ability to deal with nerves – or 'elbow' ('choking' is another way to describe it) – is essential. There are positive steps a player can take to conquer nerves and perform to his full potential. It is all bound up with attitude and concentration – keeping the mind focused on the next shot, not allowing distractions or frustrations to interfere.

Learning to concentrate

One way to release tension at the start of a game is to hit out boldly on the first few points. Relax the muscles, and concentrate on swinging powerfully through the ball. To concentrate the mind, think about breathing out forcefully on making contact with the ball. This is a habit which has led to the increase in 'grunting' on court. But you do not have to make as loud a noise as Monica Seles.

If you are nervous during a match, slow down everything you do. Breathe deeply. Take your time. Try to slow your pulse rate. Don't look outside the court. Look at the ground between points, or at your racket. Try to develop a routine to keep the mind occupied.

Have you ever watched John McEnroe at the change-over between games? He walks back to his chair very carefully, avoiding stepping on any lines, and moving straight to the sideline, before turning at right-angles to get to his chair. It is not so much a superstition for John, but a way of keeping his concentration, and avoiding eye contact with anything outside the court.

Top players use the change-overs to plan their tactics for the next game or two. They go into the next game with a game-plan already formulated, and can concentrate on playing the shots. The greatest difference in approach between professional players and club performers is in their attitude to mistakes, bad calls or other upsets.

Most club players allow themselves to be completely distracted. A bad mistake preys on their mind. Two or three points later they are still thinking back to the easy shot they missed. It is a fatal and futile habit. Top players know that what has

Opposite: John McEnroe, despite his outbursts on court, plays better when he is under pressure and has the ability to bounce back and think positively after a bad shot or line call.

gone, has gone, and there is no point dwelling on it. Mental energy is precious; it should not be wasted on thinking back to previous points.

Bad luck (like net-cords etc) and bad calls are harder to accept, but the best players take them in their stride. They accept that things will generally even up in the long run. Of course, we have all seen how even great champions can get upset by line calls, but most know how to control their emotions on court. They have learned to channel their anger into their game, rather than let it spill out.

Losing your temper on court is totally unproductive. It wastes mental energy, causes loss of control, and serves only as an encouragement to your opponent. Frustration at your own mistakes is just as damaging. If you hit a bad shot, forget it. Reverse the situation. Act as if you had hit a winner. Don't allow yourself to slump. Drooping shoulders merely send signals to your opponent that you are demoralized, and his confidence will soar without him even hitting a ball.

Always try to think positively – Bjorn Borg was a marvellous example of that. He won Wimbledon one year with a stomach muscle injury that would have caused many players to withdraw. It would have been easy for Borg to look on it as an easy way out. Some players are happy to have a ready-made excuse for losing, but not Borg. He just got on with playing, and concentrated on finding a way to overcome his injury.

Borg thought only about winning – losing never entered his mind. He was always positive in his approach. That applied to his play as much as to his mental attitude, and it is the same with most champions. The great players always react posi-

tively when they are in trouble. They never resort to pushing the ball around. They will attack the ball more aggressively when losing, and concentrate on hitting the ball cross-court rather than down the line, giving themselves more room for error.

Another example of Bjorn Borg's mental strength was his last victory at Wimbledon in 1980. In the final against John McEnroe, Borg was leading two sets to one, when the fourth set went into a tie-break. It was probably the finest ever tie-break sequence, almost every point earned with a winning shot. But after holding, and losing, several match points, Borg lost the tie-break 19-17.

At two sets all, most players in that situation would have folded. Borg had played magnificently, and had still failed to win. Everyone made McEnroe favourite to win the final set – except Borg. He concentrated his mind on getting his first serve on target and made that his priority for the fifth set. In six service games in that fifth set, Borg dropped only four points. He hardly missed a first serve. The pressure was right back on McEnroe and, inevitably, Borg went on to win the championship.

Concentration can be learned. It does come naturally to some people, but others less fortunate can acquire the ability. I had to do it. One of my daily tasks as a young player was to finish the *Daily Telegraph* newspaper crossword puzzle every day. I am not naturally good at crosswords, but I was told there were then four different compilers of the *Telegraph* puzzle, and each had his own train of thought. It was

Opposite: Andre Agassi was beaten by Andres Gomez, a lesser player, in the 1990 French Open final because Gomez was clever enough to exploit his weaknesses and lack of physical strength.

my task to learn how each compiler's mind worked, through attempting the puzzle every day, and then solving the clues would become relatively straightforward. I had to concentrate hard, and I did not always finish every clue. However, it was a great exercise in logical thinking and concentration.

Another thing I had to do every day was a memory game – Pelmanism I believe it's called. You lay out a pack of cards, face down, in a grid. Turning up two cards at a time, you have to try to find a 'pair'. The aim is to remember where every card is, so that you can locate all 26 pairs in the shortest possible time.

One trick to help concentration on the court is to number the balls you are playing with in practice with a marker pen. Then, as you practise, you try to watch each ball as it comes at you, so closely that you can read the number on it.

Another idea is to develop a verbal routine in a rally. As your opponent hits the ball you say, for example, 'Ready'. When the ball bounces on your side of the court, you say, 'Steady'. And as you make contact you say, 'Go'. It helps concentrate the mind on preparing early, and attacking the ball.

A lot of top sports people these days are using a technique called 'visualization'. It basically involves relaxing completely in a quiet spot, and then imagining watching yourself play, and win, your match. You visualize yourself hitting perfect shots, winning the points, and beating your opponent. It is a kind of mental rehearsal, and is probably most effective when performed immediately before going out to play.

Mental fitness also encompasses the ability to analyse your opponent, and identify either technical, physical, or mental weaknesses you can exploit. An example is the 1990 final of the French Open between André Agassi and Andres Gomez. On paper there is no way Gomez should have won that match. Agassi was younger, he hit the ball harder, and his ranking proved he was a better player. But Gomez knew Agassi was not actually as strong or as physically fit as he should have been. He knew he had a chance if he just kept the ball going, and waited for Agassi to blow himself out. And that is what happened.

Gomez identified and exploited the weakness. He won a Grand Slam event; the only one he is likely to win. Agassi learned from the experience; he took a couple of months off, and worked hard pumping iron in the gym. By the end of the year he was able to win the five-set matches.

A similar thing happened with Boris Becker. After two years as Wimbledon champion, he got a bit lazy, put on a bit of weight, and lost his agility. A string of opponents spotted the flaw. They moved him around the court and exploited his lack of mobility. Boris had a tough time until he recognised his problem, got back in the gym and worked harder on his fitness.

The top players are ruthless on court. They study their opponents, and work out a game plan to exploit any weakness. The club player can do the same. It is called playing smart. If you are mentally fit and clever, you always have a chance.

CHAPTER SEVEN

DIET AND NUTRITION

It does not matter how hard you train, or how fit and strong you are, if you go into a match unable to make the most of all that preparation. But that will happen if you are careless or unthinking about what and when you eat. Thirty years ago, not many players really paid much attention to their diet and nutrition. Today many top players have their own nutritionist to advise on diet, and to work out the best foods to eat at different times.

To some extent I am a believer in the adage 'a little bit of what you fancy does you good'. In other words, I'm not going to say, 'Don't eat this or that'. After all, some people thrive on foods that others find indigestible. But I do believe that there are sensible ideas to follow, particularly with regard to pre-match meals.

The most important point to remember is that emotional tension, which most players experience to some degree before a match, impairs the digestive system. When you are feeling tense, food is digested more slowly than normal. It can take four or five hours to fully empty the stomach. As you should always play on an empty stomach, it is clear that your pre-match meal should be eaten several hours before you are due to play.

When you eat too soon before playing, the general blood supply finds it tough to do two jobs at once – digesting the food, and coping with the muscular demands. One, or both, functions can be impaired. It is better to go on court feeling slightly hungry, rather than too full.

Maintaining fluid levels

Professional players who have an early morning match, are likely to have a big meal, full of carbohydrates, the previous night, and eat a very light, easily digested breakfast before playing. What they will do is to make certain that they take plenty of liquids before play. The average club player probably does not realise the importance of drinking a lot of fluid before, and during, play.

Although it obviously applies more in hot weather, it is still important to maintain fluid levels in all climates. During a closely-fought match, a player can lose several pints of liquid. That fluid must be replaced, or the result will be dehydration. The body does not function properly when it gets dehydrated. The chemical reaction within the blood cells is affected, slowing reactions, blurring the thought process, and draining the strength.

My former sister-in-law, Chris Evert, was meticulous about drinking enough liquid. In the build-up to a match, she took a large glass of water every hour. And she would drink water during every change-over on court, no matter how easy the match. The result was that even in a long three-setter, her clarity of thought and concentration was needle sharp from start to finish.

There are on the market a number of different 'electrolyte' or mineral drinks designed to replace the essential minerals lost through sweat. They can contain potassium, sodium, calcium and phosphorous among others. Some players swear by

them, but experts say that pure water is still the best drink to take – the best way to absorb the minerals into the body is naturally through food.

I think you should drink whatever you believe is best for you. There is a psychological aspect involved; if you think something is doing you good, it probably will.

Eating a balanced diet

For an athlete it is important to maintain a constant body weight. There should not be too much fluctuation. That means striking the right balance between energy output and intake. What you burn up on court must be replaced at the meal table.

The metabolic rate, ie., the rate at which the body is burning up calories, increases hugely during strenuous exercise. So the amount of food (or rather the number of calories) you need after a tough match is much greater than would be the case on a day without exercise.

A varied and balanced diet is essential. For top performance, the body needs regular supplies of protein, fat, carbohydrates, water, vitamins and minerals. In a reasonably varied diet, the body should acquire all the essential elements without special supplements. That is one reason why I do not particularly believe in rigid diets, or banning certain foods that some people may consider harmful.

For instance, in the old days, steak was the recommended food for sportsmen trying to build up strength. Nowadays, red meats are not encouraged because it is

Opposite: Chris Evert valued a healthy diet, and alwasy drank plenty of water before, during and after a match. This helped her matchplay concentration and made her needle-sharp on court.

thought that fat content leads to high blood cholesterol levels. As far as I am concerned, it you enjoy steak then have it – in moderation – but not before you play tennis. And make sure the rest of your diet is balanced with white meat, fish, and plenty of vegetables and fruits.

Pre-match meals

I am more concerned about match-day meals. It is much easier to define what is, and what is not, right before a strenuous match or practice session.

For instance, steak, or any red meat, contains a lot of fat and protein. Although they are essential components of the diet, they are slow to digest, and not the main source of energy. Carbohydrate is the main provider of energy. It is converted into glycogen by the digestive system, and becomes the primary 'fuel' for the muscles.

Most tennis players at professional level will make their pre-match meal high in carbohydrates to provide the energy. Tournament caterers are always asked to put dishes like pasta on the menu because of the high carbohydrate level. Cereals are another good source of carbohydrate. For that reason, many players will content themselves with a good breakfast as a pre-match meal.

Chris Evert, for instance, favoured a bowl of whole-grain cereal, with bananas and honey and skimmed milk; one, or two, soft-boiled eggs; and fruit juice. The cereal and fruit are a good source of complex carbohydrate, while honey is also a good energy source.

Martina Navratilova prefers corn flakes, also with skimmed milk; brown bread; and sometimes pasta with sweet potatoes and rice, if she has an afternoon match. Ivan Lendl likes a whole-grain cereal, with fruit, and toast. Mats Wilander has corn flakes, toast, fruit and fruit juice.

One or two players favour pancakes with syrup and bananas – very few will ever eat a 'fry-up' on the day of a match. Bacon, eggs, cheese etc. contain too much fat to be digested easily, especially if fried. Avoid fats if possible. Too much fat 'floods' the blood, impairing its ability to carry oxygen to the muscles.

When choosing a drink, it's worth remembering that while it is better to drink 'pure' fruit juice than 'squash', too much concentrated juice can overload the digestive system. One glass of orange juice is the equivalent of at least three whole fruit. Rather than two glasses of fruit juice, it is better to make the second a glass of water.

If you have a particularly important match to play, with a few days beforehand to prepare for it, you could try the diet routine that was first dreamed up by marathon runners. In the six days before a race, these athletes will follow a particular diet. For the first three days they will cut out all carbohydrates, but in the following three days they will follow a very high-carbohydrate diet, eating mountains of pasta, cereals and fruit. The result is that on race day they have a very high level of glycogen in the muscles, producing the energy and stamina required for the race.

It is a method not really suitable for the professional tennis player, because his best effort has to be repeated day after day for a week or more during a tournament. He does not have six days to build up to one big match. But for the club player, facing his local final, it might be worth a try.

For a general diet, on non-match days, I recommend eating what you enjoy, as long as the meals are sensibly balanced. Modern nutritionists recommend low-fat

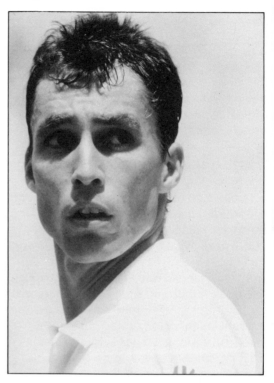

Ivan Lendl (above) favours a healthy breakfast on a match day of whole-grain cereal and fruit, whereas Martina Navratilova (opposite) has corn flakes or even pasta with sweet potatoes.

and high-fibre diets, and I would not disagree with this, but everybody is different, and I would not be dogmatic about diet. I can only say that white meats, like poultry and veal, and fish, green vegetables, potatoes, eggs, cheese, fruit and nuts should provide just about everything the body needs.

The important thing is to follow a balanced diet, to drink plenty of liquids, and to replace all the calories that are burned up during exercise. And remember to play your tennis on an empty stomach.

CHAPTER EIGHT

INJURIES

When you walk into the locker room of a top tournament, it can be a little like entering the casualty ward of a hospital – strappings, bandages and ice-packs everywhere. Some players attend post-match interviews looking like make-shift American footballers, with ice packs strapped to their shoulders, knees and arms.

Being fit does not mean that you are immune to injury. The average professional player can rarely claim to be completely 100 per cent free of physical stresses and strains. They learn to cope with minor problems. Above all, they try to avoid injury. Prevention is better than cure, and the same principle applies to the club player. Sensible precautions are always better than costly remedies.

I stressed in an early chapter the importance of warming up before training or playing. That is the best protection there is against muscle damage in ordinary exercise, but injuries will still occur under the stress of hard competitive play. The trick is to recognise the extent of the damage and treat it quickly; identify the cause and try to remove it; and do everything possible to prevent a reoccurrence. The majority of injuries to tennis players are caused by overuse. It is a non-contact sport, so injuries should be relatively straightforward.

My brother John experienced a lot of arm trouble as a young player. One consultant even said that he had the arm of a 40-year-old – and he was barely 20 at the time! But it wasn't until much later that he discovered the cause of those problems. While in Australia, John visited the gymnasium used by former Australian star Margaret (Smith) Court. He had a work-out on the weights, and discovered to his shame that he could lift only about half the poundage regularly hoisted aloft by the former Wimbledon Ladies Champion.

John found that his shoulder muscles had never been developed properly to cope with the stresses of serving and hitting over-heads. All the power he mustered was produced by the arm and wrist – hence the injury problems. Once he built up his shoulder muscles, he found that he had hardly any further arm trouble.

That's one example of injury prevention: making sure that one part of the body is not over-stressed because of weakness elsewhere. There are other more obvious precautions you can take to guard against simple injuries – taking care over clothing and shoes for match-play and training, for instance. Clothes should not be too loose – nor too tight. If you are training or playing in very cold weather, it is better to wear two or three thin layers, rather than one heavy, thick layer. The thin layers allow more air to circulate, and provide better insulation. The American player Barbara Potter caused a stir at Wimbledon one year by stripping off her shirt on court and putting on a fresh one, but she was only being sensible. The men have been doing it for years. Sweat-soaked clothes should be changed as often as is practical.

Be aware of court surfaces, and adapt your technique accordingly. For example, on grass, artificial grass and clay courts, it is possible to 'slide' into shots. However, try to do the same thing on cement, or indoor carpet courts, and you risk knee and ankle damage. At my clubs I insist on the wearing of 'slick' shoes on the indoor courts. They are custom-made for carpet surfaces, with smooth soles without any tread or ribbing.

If you are doing a lot of running, stick to grass surfaces, and even then make sure that there is sufficient padding in your shoes to absorb the shock. Try to avoid running uphill or downhill, which can cause problems. Running uphill can strain the calf muscles and achilles tendons; running downhill may lead to shin-splints.

Common tennis injuries

Tennis elbow

You don't have to play tennis to suffer from tennis elbow, but many players do. It is a common problem which can become a chronic condition if not treated early, and if the cause is not removed. Tennis elbow is inflammation on the outside of the elbow joint where the muscles of the forearm are attached to the joint. The pain is felt particularly on the backhand, because the muscles involved are those that bend the wrist back. Applying ice to the inflamed area helps, but rest is basically the only cure, although injections can help severe cases. There are also special supports that you can buy from sports shops, or sports injury clinics, which alleviate discomfort.

The cause of tennis elbow often lies with the racket. The grip may be too big, or too small. The racket may be too heavy. It is possibly strung too tightly. Vibration in the racket frame is also damaging, and some rackets are worse than others in this respect. There are vibration 'dampers' you can fit on the strings to absorb some of the shock.

The cause will vary with every case of tennis elbow, so try to pinpoint the problem as soon as you experience any pain. The longer you leave it, the more likely you are to have a chronic problem.

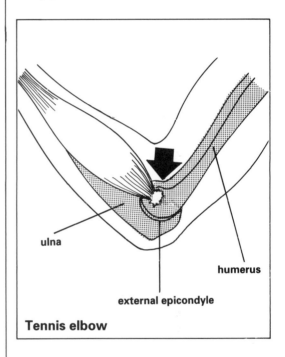

Tennis elbow

ulna

humerus

external epicondyle

Golfers elbow

Golfers elbow is the 'complement' of tennis elbow. It involves pain on the inside of the elbow joint, caused by inflammation of the muscles of the forearm where they attach to the bone. The difference is that the muscles control the inward movement of the wrist, and discomfort is felt on the forehand shots and service. Cause and prevention, as well as cure, are all similar to those for tennis elbow. If you experience this injury, seek professional advice.

Shin-splints

This is an 'over-use' injury, caused by constant pounding on unforgiving hard courts. The injury is an inflammation of the lower leg muscles where they are attached to the bone, most commonly to the inner part of the tibia. Once again, ice packs and rest are the best cure.

For prevention, get a qualified physio to watch you in action. Shin-splints can be caused by faulty running technique – running with the toes pointing out, for example; and aggravated by improper footwear. Occasionally, special padded inserts in the shoes can help.

Severe pain in the shins may not be caused by muscle damage. If the pain is very localized, there could be a stress fracture of the bone. This is not uncommon in players who overdo their training, or who suddenly step-up their mileage. Complete rest is the only cure and can take up to ten to twelve weeks. Prevention is better, so build up slowly in training and avoid running much on hard surfaces.

Achilles tendon

Inflammation of the achilles tendon occurs frequently when tennis players train very hard and play long hours on hard courts. Curiously, running on very soft surfaces –

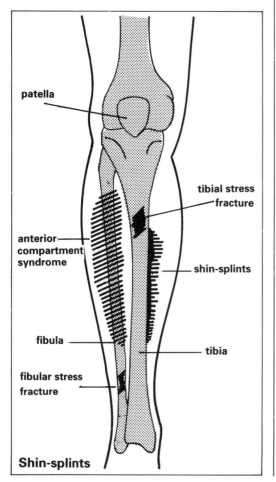

Shin-splints

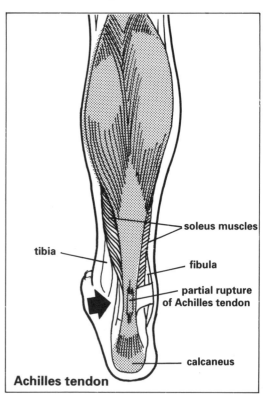

Achilles tendon

such as the beach – can also harm the achilles tendon. Occasionally, sudden stressful movements on court can tear or even rupture the achilles. There is not a lot you can do to prevent this, but wearing shock-absorbent heel pads, about 1cm/½in thick, in the shoes can help prevent inflammation.

Shoulder injuries

The shoulder is a very complex joint, and it is common for tennis players to damage one of the rotator cuff tendons which hold the upper arm in the shoulder socket. The tendon becomes inflamed, and in over-arm action, it 'snags' on the bone.

The greatest danger is in trying to hit serves or over-heads before the shoulder joint is properly warmed-up. More than any other shot, never try to serve or smash before thoroughly warming and stretching the shoulders.

Rotator cuff injuries are very difficult to treat; once more, rest is the best cure, along with the regular application of ice. Never continue playing if the shoulder is painful,

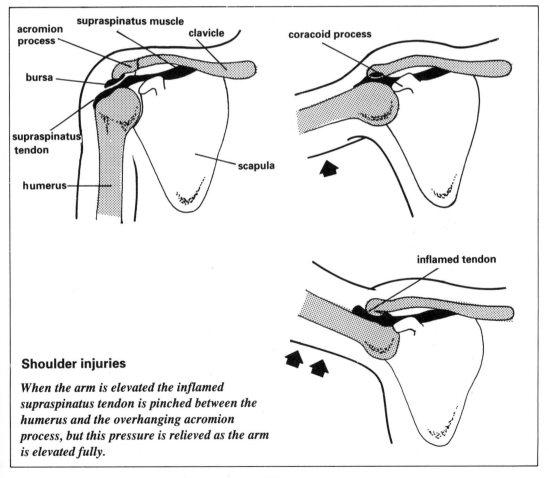

Shoulder injuries

When the arm is elevated the inflamed supraspinatus tendon is pinched between the humerus and the overhanging acromion process, but this pressure is relieved as the arm is elevated fully.

as chronic damage to the tendons can be caused if pain is ignored. Warming up is the best prevention. But it also helps to develop the shoulder muscles to support the joint.

Summary

Obviously, there are many more injuries that can be suffered in training, or on court. Pulled muscles, damaged knee ligaments or cartilages (I know all about those) and strained backs, to name but a few.

If you have an injury, get it treated by an expert. Early diagnosis and treatment can prevent long-term problems. There are more specialized sports-injury clinics opening up nowadays, staffed by highly-trained physiotherapists with the latest hi-tech equipment. Find a good clinic, and trust their advice. Above all, don't try to return from injury too soon. Make sure that you are 100 per cent recovered before you set foot again on a tennis court. Ask about alternative exercises you can do if you have to rest an injury. Cycling and swimming are often recommended for maintaining general fitness during a lay-off. But as I said before – prevention is better than cure.

Index

Numerals in *italics* refer to illustrations